Discover the
Dinosaurs

DINOSAURS IN THE SKY

By Joseph Staunton
Illustrated by Luis Rey

amicus

mankato, minnesota

Published by Amicus
P.O. Box 1329, Mankato, Minnesota 56002

Printed in the United States of America at Corporate Graphics,
in North Mankato, Minnesota.

Published by arrangement with the Watts Publishing Group LTD, London.

Library of Congress Cataloging-in-Publication Data
Staunton, Joseph.
  Dinosaurs in the sky / by Joseph Staunton.
      p. cm. -- (Discover the dinosaurs)
  Includes index.
  Summary: "Profiles flying dinosaurs from the Devonian, Triassic, Jurassic, and
Cretaceous periods"--Provided by publisher.
  ISBN 978-1-60753-108-1 (library binding)
  1. Pterosauria--Juvenile literature. 2. Birds, Fossil--Juvenile literature. I. Title.
  QE862.P7S73 2011
  567.918--dc22
                                                   2009029977

Editor: Jeremy Smith
Design: Nicola Liddiard
Art director: Jonathan Hair
Consultant: Dougal Dixon MSc
Illustrations: Copyright © Luis Rey 2009

1209
32010

9 8 7 6 5 4 3 2 1

Contents

A World of Dinosaurs

Dinosaurs were the most famous group of animals to **evolve** in **prehistoric** times. Some were huge, but others were small and could glide in the air. At the same time there were true flying reptiles called **pterosaurs**, and also the first birds. The **fossils** of all these different flying animals are found in rocks dating from the **periods** shown below.

A Changing World

The Earth in the past looked very different from how it looks now. Before dinosaur times all the continents were jammed together as one big landmass. During dinosaur times this landmass broke up into the individual continents that started to move away from each other. The seas between the continents opened up. Oceans in other parts of the globe closed. Above all these changing landscapes and oceans, there flew all kinds of strange winged animals.

Fossil Flyers

The most common fossils are those of animals that lived in the water. Animals that lived on land, such as dinosaurs, rarely fossilized since their bodies rotted away in the sun or were eaten by other animals. Lightweight animals, such as flying creatures, hardly ever fossilized on land. Their remains are most often found in **sediments** laid down in the sea or in the quiet waters of lakes.

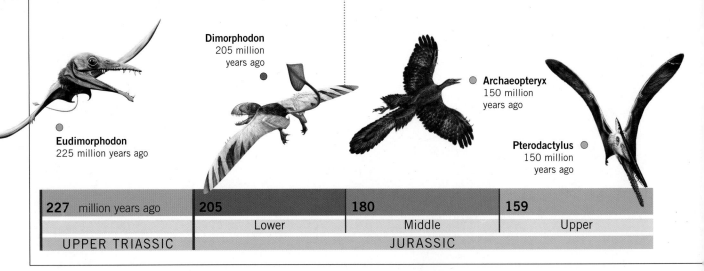

Dimorphodon
205 million
years ago

Archaeopteryx
150 million
years ago

Eudimorphodon
225 million years ago

Pterodactylus
150 million
years ago

227 million years ago	205	180	159
	Lower	Middle	Upper
UPPER TRIASSIC		JURASSIC	

Triassic World Most of Earth's land is joined together in a single supercontinent.

Cretaceous World The supercontinent starts to split up.

Destruction!

Then, 65 million years ago the dinosaurs were all wiped out. Scientists think that this may have been caused by the impact of an enormous **meteorite** that smashed into the Earth. This disaster also wiped out all the flying reptiles that lived alongside them. Once the Earth recovered and the **mammals** took over the place of the dinosaurs as the main land-living animals, the sky was full of flying creatures again.

A Lasting Legacy

The most successful flying animals of today are birds that evolved from the dinosaurs. Scientists can tell this from the fossils that have been found. The earliest known is *Archaeopteryx*. This was a bird with wings and flight **feathers**, but it still had a dinosaur's toothy jaws, a long bony tail, and clawed fingers. From later rocks we find all kinds of other animals that share dinosaur and bird features. Although the dinosaurs died out, their descendants lived on.

Microraptor
120 million years ago

Caulkicephalus
125 million years ago

Pterodaustro
110 million years ago

Tapejara
100 million years ago

Quetzalcoatlus
65 million years ago

Pteranodon
90 million years ago

144	98	65
Lower	Upper	
CRETACEOUS		

Caulkicephalus (CORL-kee-KEPHER-luss)

Caulkicephalus (caulk head) was first discovered on a small island off Britain called the Isle of Wight. A skeleton, teeth, and part of the bird's **skull** were discovered in 1997.

Dino-Data

Wingspan	6.5 feet (2 m)
Weight	3.3 lbs (1.5 kg)
Length	3.2 feet (1 m)

⬇ WINGSPAN

Scientists have been able to work out the **wingspan** of this pterosaur from fossil remains. It would have had a gigantic wingspan of around 6.5 feet (2 m).

⬇ MARSH LIFE

A *Caulkicephalus* fossil found in the United States was discovered next to some fossilized mussels. This suggests that *Caulkicephalus* lived around rivers or wet **marsh** land.

⬇ SHARP TEETH

Caulkicephalus had a colorful **beak** crammed full of teeth of many different sizes. At the front were **fang**-like weapons, used to snatch fish from the top of the water.

ARCHAEOPTERYX (ARE-kee-OP-ter-iks)

Archaeopteryx (ancient wing) is the earliest and most **primitive** bird known. The first complete **specimen** was discovered in 1861. This bird lived in the Late **Jurassic period** on islands that make up modern Germany.

LIKE A DINOSAUR?

Despite looking like a bird, *Archaeopteryx* had more in common with small dinosaurs. It had jaws with sharp teeth, a long, bony tail, and deadly claws on its **forelimbs**.

Dino-Data

Wingspan	1 foot (0.3 m)
Weight	1.1 lbs (5 kg)
Length	1.6 feet (0.5 m)

🐾 FIRST FEATHERS

Fossils of *Archaeopteryx have* been found showing impressions of feathers. They suggest that *Archaeopteryx* was the first flying bird, and a link between dinosaurs and modern birds.

🐾 HUNTER

Archaeopteryx had long legs and large feet, which suggest it spent much of its time on the ground. It probably searched for food in trees, shrubs, and open ground, seizing small **prey** with its jaws or claws.

EUDIMORPHODON (YOU-die-MOR-fo-don)

Eudimorphodon (true *Dimorphodon*) was a flying reptile that lived in the Upper **Triassic period**. It is one of the earliest pterosaurs that existed. The first fossil of *Eudimorphodon* was discovered by Mario Pandolfi near Bergamo, Italy in 1973.

♧ STEERING

At the end of its long bony tail *Eudimorphodon* had a diamond-shaped flap. This may have been used to change direction while *Eudimorphodon* was in flight.

Dino-Data

Wingspan	3.2 feet (1 m)
Weight	1.1 lbs (0.5 kg)
Length	1.9 feet (0.6 m)

☙ WINGS

Eudimorphodon had a large wingspan and was one of the largest Triassic pterosaurs. Experts think it may have had the ability to flap its primitive wings to soar through the air.

☙ TEETH

Eudimorphodon had over 100 teeth packed into a jaw only 2.3 inches (6 cm) long. The front teeth faced outward while the back ones had tiny hooks facing in opposite directions, ideal for hooking prey from the water.

DIMORPHODON (die-MOR-fo-don)

Dimorphodon (two-formed teeth) was a medium-sized pterosaur from the Lower Jurassic period. It was named by **paleontologist** Richard Owen in 1859.

⬇ BIG HEAD

Dimorphodon had a huge head for its size. It was 8.6 inches (22 cm) long, with toothed jaws, that would have looked similar to the beak of a puffin. Its size may have been used by the male to compete for female attention.

Dino-Data

Wingspan	3.9 feet (1.2 m)
Weight	1 lb (0.45 kg)
Length	1.9 feet (0.6 m)

⬇ EARLY FIND

The first *Dimorphodon* fossil remains were found in England by Mary Anning, at Lyme Regis in Dorset in 1828. This region of Britain is now a **World Heritage Site**, and is known as the Jurassic Coast.

⬇ CLUMSY LEGS

Like most other pterosaurs, *Dimorphodon's* legs sprawled out at the sides. This meant that it would have been clumsy on land. Instead of walking when not flying, perhaps it hung from cliffs or branches using its powerful claws.

QUETZALCOATLUS (KWET-zal-co-AT-lus)

Quetzalcoatlus (named after the Aztec feathered serpent god, Quetzalcoatl) was a pterosaur from the Late **Cretaceous period**. It lived in North America and was one of the largest-known flying animals of all time. The first fossils were discovered in Texas in 1971.

⬇ LIGHT FLIGHT

Quetzalcoatlus had a wingspan of nearly 36 feet (11 m). Despite its size, it probably weighed only about 190 lbs (86 kg). It had hollow bones and a small body, with a long neck and slender jaws.

⬇ ALL FOURS

Although *Quetzalcoatlus* spent time soaring through the sky, scientists think it also spent a lot of time on all fours on the ground. It may have hunted in this way too, like herons do today.

⬇ BIG BEAK

Quetzalcoatlus belonged to a family of pterosaurs called the *Azhdarchidae*. This group was all toothless, and had long, thin beaks and stiff necks up to 10 feet (3 m) long.

Dino-Data

Wingspan	36 feet (11 m)
Weight	190 lbs (86 kg)
Length	16.4 feet (5 m)

TAPEJARA (TOP-ay-HAR-ah)

Tapejara (old one) was a Brazilian pterosaur that lived during the Cretaceous period. Its most striking feature was its huge, brightly colored crest.

🦶 SIZE

There were many different **species** of *Tapejara*. *Tapejara imperator* was the largest, with a wingspan of up to 19.6 feet (6 m).

Dino-Data

Wingspan	19.6 feet (6 m)
Weight	20 lbs (9 kg)
Length	Up to 19.6 feet (6 m)

🦶 CURVED BEAK

Tapejara had a beak that curved downward. Experts think it used this to pluck fish from the sea.

⟲ GREAT CREST

Tapejara imperator had a gigantic crest that took up most of this pterosaur's huge skull. This colorful crest was probably used by males to attract mates.

PTERANODON (TER-ANN-oh-don)

Pteranodon (toothless wing) lived in the Upper Cretaceous period in North America. This mighty pterosaur had a wingspan of over 23 feet (7 m).

↻ NO TEETH

Unlike earlier pterosaurs, such as *Rhamphorhynchus* and *Pterodactylus*, *Pteranodon* had a toothless beak, much like that of a modern bird.

Dino-Data

Wingspan	25 feet (7.6 m)
Weight	17.6 lbs (8 kg)
Length	Up to 19.6 feet (6 m)

🐾 FUR AND FLIGHT

Pteranodon could flap its wings and fly with power. It flew long distances using large, lightweight wings. *Pteranodon* had a large brain, good eyesight, and a light covering of fur.

🐾 DIET

Although it had no teeth, *Pteranodon* was a **carnivore**. It may have hunted like modern-day pelicans, scooping fish out of the water and swallowing them whole.

MICRORAPTOR (mi-CRO-rap-tore)

Microraptor (small one who seizes) was a type of small dinosaur from the Lower Cretaceous period. Over 20 fossils have been recovered from Liaoning, China.

🐾 MAKING LINKS

Like *Archaeopteryx*, *Microraptor* provides important evidence of the link between birds and dinosaurs. Its feet suggest that it could grasp branches and therefore live in trees, like most birds. Feathers on its legs suggest that the **hind limbs** were wings as well.

Dino-Data

Wingspan	1.9 feet (0.6 m)
Weight	2.2 lbs (1 kg)
Length	2.7 feet (0.83 m)

⬇ DEADLY CLAWS

Microraptor was a type of
dromaeosaur—a small,
fast-running carnivorous
dinosaur with a sickle-like
claw on its middle toe.
The creature belongs to a
group of dinosaurs called
theropods—two-legged
predators with sharp teeth.

⬇ GLIDER

Microraptor would not have
been able to take off from the
ground in the way birds do.
It couldn't lift its front
wings high enough off the
ground. Scientists think
that this dinosaur
"flew" by gliding
from the tops of
tall trees.

PTERODACTYLUS (TER-oh-DACK-till-us)

Pterodactylus (wing finger) was a small pterosaur that lived during the Late Jurassic period. It was the first flying reptile to be identified by scientists. Fossils have been found in Tanzania, England, France, and Germany.

Dino-Data

Wingspan	2.4 feet (0.75 m)
Weight	14 oz (0.4 kg)
Length	1.3 feet (0.4 m)

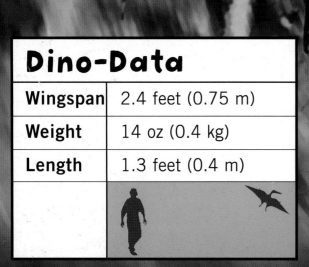

✋ HAIR AND FEET

In 1998, the discovery of a single fossil in Germany told scientists more about this pterosaur. It had a crest on its skull, a mane of hair down the back of its neck, and **webbed** feet.

✋ LAKE LIFE

Pterodactylus lived by the shores of Jurassic lakes. Scientists think that it also laid eggs there, like modern turtles do today.

PTERODAUSTRO (TER-oh-DAWS-tro)

Pterodaustro (southern wing) was a Cretaceous pterosaur from South America. It had a large wingspan, a colorful appearance, and a mouth packed with bristles.

⬥ IN THE PINK

Pterodaustro is often called the "flamingo pterosaur." This is because, like a flamingo, it fed by filtering tiny creatures from shallow water. It may even have had a flamingo's pink color, due to the food it ate.

⬥ BASKET BEAK

Pterodaustro probably waded in shallow water, like flamingos, to catch food, or skimmed over the water while flying, using its beak like a basket to sift food from the water.

Dino-Data

Wingspan	4.2 feet (1.3 m)
Weight	1.1 lbs (0.5 kg)
Length	1.9 feet (0.6 m)

⬇ BRISTLE TEETH

Pterodaustro had about 1,000 bristles instead of teeth. It used these to strain **crustaceans**, **plankton**, **algae**, and other small creatures from the water in the same way that some whales do today.

Quiz— Look back through the book to find the answer.

CAULKICEPHALUS (CORL-kee-KEPHER-luss)

- Where was *Caulkicephalus* found?
- When was it discovered?
- How do we know that it lived near water?
- Did *Caulkicephalus* have a tail?

ARCHAEOPTERYX (ARE-kee-OP-ter-iks)

- What does *Archaeopteryx* mean?
- Was its tail like a bird's or a dinosaur's?
- How big was *Archaeopteryx*?

EUDIMORPHODON (YOU-die-MOR-fo-don)

- What did *Eudimorphodon* have on the end of its tail?
- How many kinds of teeth did it have?
- What were the teeth used for?
- Who found the first *Eudimorphodon*?

DIMORPHODON (die-MOR-fo-don)

- How did *Dimorphodon* attract mates?
- Who found the first *Dimorphodon* fossil?
- How did it hang from cliffs and branches?
- Where was the first *Dimorphodon* fossil found?

QUETZALCOATLUS (KWET-zal-co-AT-lus)

- *Quetzalcoatlus* is named after a god from which country?
- Did it hunt in the air or on the ground?
- Was its neck long or short?

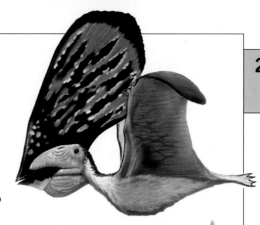

TAPEJARA (TOP-ay-HAR-ah)

- 🐾 What did *Tapejara* have on its head?
- 🐾 Which was the biggest species of *Tapejara*?
- 🐾 In which country was it found?
- 🐾 How big was *Tapejara's* wingspan?

PTERANODON (TER-ANN-oh-don)

- 🐾 Was *Pteranodon* bigger or smaller than *Quetzalcoatlus*?
- 🐾 What kind of teeth did it have?
- 🐾 What was *Pteranodon's* skin covered with?
- 🐾 How did it feed?

MICRORAPTOR (mi-CRO-rap-tore)

- 🐾 *Microraptor* is the only dinosaur in this book. True or false?
- 🐾 How many wings did *Microraptor* have?
- 🐾 How many fossils of *Microraptor* have been found?
- 🐾 What dinosaur group did *Microraptor* belong to?

PTERODACTYLUS (TER-oh-DACK-till-us)

- 🐾 What does *Pterodactylus* mean?
- 🐾 Where have its fossils been found?
- 🐾 What kind of feet did it have?
- 🐾 Did *Pterodactylus* lay eggs?

PTERODAUSTRO (TER-oh-DAWS-tro)

- 🐾 How did *Pterodaustro* catch its food?
- 🐾 What color do we think *Pterodaustro* was?
- 🐾 Did it have teeth?
- 🐾 What modern bird was *Pterodaustro* like?

Glossary

Algae: Very primitive plants, including seaweed.

Beak: The hard part of a bird's mouth.

Carnivore: An animal that feeds on meat.

Cretaceous period: A period of the Earth's history from 144–65 million years ago.

Crustacean: A group of small, joint-legged water animals with no backbone, that include shrimps.

Dinosaurs: A group of land-living reptiles that were the most important land animals of the Triassic, Jurassic, and Cretaceous Periods. They did not swim and hardly any of them flew. In this book, only *Microraptor* is a true dinosaur.

Dromaeosaur: One of a group of small, fast dinosaurs that killed their prey with a sharp claw on the foot.

Evolve: To change from one form to another over time and over many generations.

Fang: A pointed tooth.

Feather: A lightweight, branching scale growing from the skin of an animal and used to keep it warm or to help it to fly.

Forelimbs: Front legs.

Fossil: The remains of a prehistoric animal or plant, that has been turned to stone and preserved for millions of years.

Hind limbs: Back legs.

Jurassic period: A period of Earth's history from 205–144 million years ago.

Mammal: An animal that gives birth to live young and feeds them on its own milk.

Marsh: An area of wet land, full of mud and water.

Meteorite: A lump of rock floating in space that can sometimes fall through the atmosphere and crash into the Earth.

Paleontologist: A person who studies fossils and other ancient life forms.

Period: A division of time distinguished by the kinds of animals and plants that lived then. A period usually lasts for tens of millions of years.

Plankton: Tiny living things that float in the water.

Predator: A hunting animal.

Prehistoric: Before written history.

Prey: An animal that is hunted for food.

Primitive: Not very advanced.

Pterosaur: A kind of flying reptile from the age of the dinosaurs.

Sediment: Mineral or organic matter deposited by water, air or ice.

Skull: The bones of the head.

Species: A group of animals or plants that have the same appearance as one another, and can breed with one another.

Specimen: A particular thing that can be studied.

Theropod: A group of dinosaurs that includes all the meat eaters.

Triassic period: A period of Earth's history from 251–205 million years ago.

Webbed: Having flaps of skin between the toes to help in swimming. A duck has webbed feet.

Wingspan: The size of a winged animal, measured from wingtip to wingtip when the wings are outstretched.

World Heritage Site: A place of either cultural or physical significance, nominated by the World Heritage Committee.

Earth's Time Line

The history of the Earth dates back over 4 billion years. Scientists divide this time into periods. The earliest period of time is the Cambrian period. Dinosaurs appeared on Earth from the Triassic to the Cretaceous periods. Mammals, including humans, appeared in the Quarternary period.

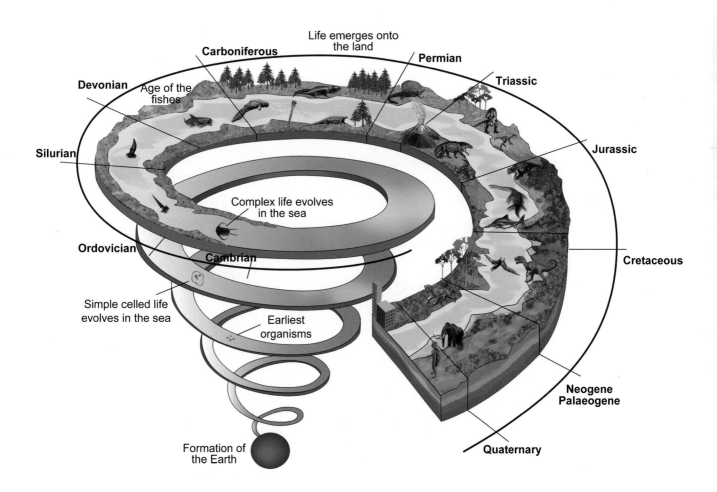

Index